Disney's Year Book

1990

Disney's Year Book

1990

GROLIER ENTERPRISES INC.
Danbury, Connecticut

ISBN: 0-7172-8242-2
ISSN: 0273-1274

Illustration Credits and Acknowledgments

6—Culver Pictures; 8—The Granger Collection; 10—© R. Maiman—Sygma; 11—© R. Maiman—Sygma; 24—© E. R. Degginger; 25—© James L. Castner; 26—© 1985 K. G. Preston-Marfhan—Discover Publications; 27—© 1985 K. G. Preston-Marfhan—Discover Publications; 28—© James L. Castner; 29—© Jane Burton—Bruce Coleman Inc.; 30—© Joseph MacNally—Sygma; 31—© The Walt Disney Company; 32—© Henson Associates, Inc.; 33—© 1989 The Walt Disney Company; 53—© Kevin Schafer—Tom Stack & Associates; 54—© Stephen J. Krasemann—DRK Photo; 55T—© Rod Planck—Tom Stack & Associates; 55B—© Dwight R. Kuhn; 68T—© 1989 Children's Television Workshop. Used Courtesy Sesame Street Magazine; 68B—© 1989 Erika Stone; 69—© 1988 Michael Greco—Picture Group; 70—© Richard Hutchings—Photo Researchers, Inc.; 71—© Al Freni—Life Magazine. © Time Inc.; 72T—*Hot Pursuit* by Kees Moerbeek & Carla Dijs © 1987 by Intervisual Communications, Inc., published by Price/Stern/Sloan Publishers Inc.; 72B—*Lavinia's Cottage* © 1982 by John S. Goodall, a Margaret K. McElderry Book, Atheneum 1983 New York; 73—*The Human Body* by Jonathan Miller, © 1983 by Dark Horse Productions Limited, published by Viking Penguin Inc. New York; 74–77—© David MacDonald—Animals Animals; 90—© Tom Ives; 91—The Granger Collection; 92—Ronald C. Modra—Sports Illustrated. © Time Inc.; 93—AP/Wide World.

Contents

The sight of the U.S. flag through the smoke of battle inspired "The Star-Spangled Banner."

Stars & Stripes

The year 1989 marked the 175th birthday of a song most Americans know well—"The Star-Spangled Banner." And the story of how this song was written is an exciting one.

The story takes place during the War of 1812, a war between the United States and Britain. In September, 1814, a British fleet sailed to attack Fort McHenry, which guarded the port city of Baltimore, Maryland.

Just before the attack, a man named Francis Scott Key went out to the fleet. He hoped to win the release of an American prisoner. And he did. But because he knew of the British plans, he was held on a prisoner-exchange boat under British guard while the attack took place.

All through the night of September 13, 1814, Key watched the battle. From time to time, he glimpsed the American flag that flew over the fort. As long as he could see the flag, he knew that the Americans hadn't surrendered.

By morning, fog and smoke made it hard to see the fort and its flag. Key peered into the mist. Suddenly the foggy curtain parted, and he saw the flag.

Key was so inspired that he immediately

In 1814 the British also attacked and burned Washington, D.C., the U.S. capital. The War of 1812 ended four months after that attack.

began writing the verses we know so well today: *"O say can you see by the dawn's early light . . ."*

Later, Key's words were set to a popular tune of the time. The song quickly became a national favorite. And in 1931, "The Star-Spangled Banner" became the national anthem of the United States.

FLAG FACTS

The first U.S. flag was adopted in 1777. Did you know that the flag has changed many times since then?

The first flag had thirteen stripes and thirteen stars—one for each of the original states. The white stripes stood for liberty. The red ground was taken from the British flag. And the stars stood for the Union.

Two stripes and two stars were added when Vermont and Kentucky joined the Union. And this was the flag (shown above) that was Key's "star-spangled banner" in 1814.

As more states joined the Union, people saw that there would soon be too many stripes. The flag would look like a pin-striped shirt! The solution was a flag with a star for each state but just the original thirteen stripes.

The last star was added in 1960, when Hawaii became a state.

BATMANIA

In 1989 people went bats—over Batman, one of the most famous comic-book heroes of all time. There were two reasons. The first was a new movie about this masked crime-fighter. The second was a birthday: the 50th anniversary of Batman's first comic-book adventure.

Batman's fans know his legend by heart. By day he's a millionaire named Bruce Wayne. By night he wears a bat-mask and cape to battle criminals—including the evil Joker. Batman's adventures have appeared in many forms, from the original comic books of 1939 to a popular TV series. The film *Batman* was one of 1989's biggest hits. And sales of Batman comics, toys, and other items boomed. On Batman's 50th birthday, "Batmania" swept the land!

From comics to clothes, items featuring Batman and the evil Joker were the rage in 1989.

The Sorcerer's Apprentice

The wizard Yen Sid was bored. Even working his favorite spells hadn't been fun.

He watched his young helper, Mickey, fill the huge well in the workroom with buckets of water. It might be fun to give Mickey a scare, he thought. So he made a bat appear.

Mickey watched the bat become a beautiful green butterfly, then disappear. He wished he could make magic like that. But Yen Sid wouldn't let him try.

Still bored, the wizard decided to go out. He left his magic hat behind.

"It's not fair," Mickey thought. "All I do is work. I want to make magic, too!"

Mickey looked at Yen Sid's tall, pointed hat. He knew the hat had great powers.

"Here's my chance!" Mickey realized. He put the hat on and waited for something terrible to happen. Nothing did.

Mickey saw an old broom leaning against the wall. And he had a wonderful idea.

Trying to remember what Yen Sid did, he waved his arms at the broom.

The broom began to glow. It started to shiver. Mickey waved again.

The broom had come to life. Mickey was proud of himself. Why, he was every bit as good a wizard as Yen Sid!

Mickey told the broom to walk, so the broomstraws separated into two fat feet. The broom took a few wobbly steps.

Mickey gave his next command, and two thick arms with strong hands popped out from the broom handle. Mickey ordered the broom to pick up two buckets, then led it up the stairs to the fountain and pointed.

Obediently, the broom filled the buckets
and followed Mickey back down to the well.
At Mickey's signal, the broom poured the
water into the huge vat.

Back and forth from the fountain to the
well Mickey skipped, with the broom tagging
along, faithfully doing all the work.

When Mickey was sure the broom knew
what to do, he plopped down in a chair to
dream about what magic he would do next.

Suddenly Mickey found himself drifting
skyward. Stars winked merrily at him, and

he winked back. Soon he was standing on a high cliff. The planets whirled past in the sky, and a comet flashed by. Mickey brought the comet swooping toward him, then sent it speeding away.

At the base of the cliff was a pounding ocean. Mickey waved his arms and huge waves splashed against the cliff.

The waves came higher and closer.
Suddenly one big wave got Mickey all wet.

He shivered—and woke up!

The cliff and ocean were gone. But there
was water everywhere!

While Mickey had been dreaming, the
broom had been working. Now the well was
overflowing.

Mickey fell into the water. Gasping and spluttering, he grabbed a bucket, but the broom just dragged him through the water and tossed him into the well, too!

Then Mickey tried saying magic words to break the spell. "Abracadabra! Alakazoola! Famitz and grimble!" he cried. It didn't work.

Suddenly Mickey saw an ax. He grabbed it and made his way outside to the fountain where the broom was working. *Chop! Chop!* Soon the broom was a pile of splinters.

Mickey walked back into the cave and shut the door. Then he heard a loud noise. Hardly daring to breathe, he peeked outside.

Mickey was horrified. Every splinter had become a broom. Every broom had two buckets. And they were all marching his way! Mickey slammed the door, but the brooms pushed it open. Broom after broom tramped over him, marching down the stairs.

The water rose higher and higher as the
brooms emptied bucket after bucket into the
overflowing well.

An open book of spells drifted past Mickey.
He scrambled onto it, looking for a spell—
any spell—to stop the brooms. But he
couldn't read the strange words.

The water whirled Mickey around in
circles. The brooms kept marching. All
seemed lost. And then . . .

There stood Yen Sid, at the top of the
stairs. Slowly, silently, he walked down.
With each step the wizard took, the water
pulled back.

Then Yen Sid raised his arms and the water
disappeared, dumping Mickey on the floor.

Mickey looked sheepishly at the wizard.
Yen Sid said nothing. Feeling ashamed,
Mickey took off the pointed hat and handed it
to him. Still, the wizard was silent.

Nervously, Mickey picked up his buckets and crept quietly toward the door.

Yen Sid picked up the broom and aimed it at Mickey. Then—*whack!*—he smacked Mickey in the seat. Mickey flew out the door.

As the wizard watched Mickey go, he smiled. Mickey had learned an important lesson. And as for himself, why, he certainly wasn't bored anymore!

Hide and Seek

Look closely at these pictures—the
animals are wearing disguises! By looking
like something that they're not, animals can
fool their enemies. And that helps them
survive.

Some animals fool their enemies by scaring

them. The swallowtail caterpillar on the opposite page looks like a monster with big, bulging eyes. But the "eyes" are really just spots on its back! When a hungry bird approaches, the caterpillar puffs up that part of its body—and the startled bird flies away.

Other animals try to blend in with their surroundings. Look carefully at the picture below. One of the leaves isn't a leaf at all— it's an insect called a katydid. There are many kinds of katydids. Some look like green leaves. Others look like dry, papery, dead

leaves. Still another katydid's disguise includes veins and ragged edges, just like the veins and ragged edges of leaves.

The South African toad grasshopper, below, has a very clever disguise. This little insect has all the markings of quartz stone. It even has the dark veining and shiny highlights that are typical of quartz. When the tiny grasshopper crouches down among the rocks, it seems to be just another pebble. An enemy may pass within inches of the grasshopper and never even know that it is

there. This type of disguise is known as
mimicry. And like the little grasshopper,
many insects are masters of mimicry.

The African mantis, above, wears a colorful
pink and green pattern that makes it look
just like a flower. This insect's disguise
serves double duty. It helps the mantis hide
from its enemies. But the mantis is also a
predator—it catches and eats other insects.
And when the mantis perches among flowers,

nectar-loving insects may mistake it for one of the blooms and be drawn to it. Then they may become dinner for the mantis!

The walking stick, above, is a common insect. But if you haven't looked carefully, you may never have seen one. That's because the walking stick looks exactly like a twig. During the day, this insect "hides" by hanging motionless in a tree or a bush. It's almost impossible to see. But at night, under the cover of darkness, the walking stick moves from its perch. It walks about the branches, enjoying a tasty dinner of leaves.

When it comes to disguises, the animals of the sea are just as clever as the animals of the land. And one of the best disguises of all is that of the glass catfish, below. The body and fins of this fish are almost as transparent as water. In fact, you can see the fish's internal organs. The glass catfish spends most of its time hanging motionless in the water. Unless you look very closely, it's hard to tell that the fish is there at all.

Disney Magic

This Chicago back alley is one of the scenes from classic films in The Great Movie Ride.

Did you ever wonder how cartoon characters like Mickey Mouse come to life on the screen? How moviemakers create special effects? What it would be like to see yourself on television?

You can find out—and have a lot of fun—at the new Disney-MGM Studios Theme Park. The park opened in 1989 at Walt Disney World in Florida. It's more than a theme park—it's a real movie and TV studio. Here are some of the sights:

Make Room for Miss Piggy

The family of Disney characters welcomed some new members in 1989: Miss Piggy, Kermit the Frog, and the rest of the Muppet troupe. The Muppets were created by puppeteer Jim Henson in the 1950's. They have starred on TV, in movies, and in animated cartoons. Now The Walt Disney Company owns the famous puppet characters. They'll continue their careers alongside Mickey Mouse, Donald Duck, and other Disney stars.

• The Great Movie Ride carries you right into movies of the past. Life-size animated figures appear in scenes from *Mary Poppins*, *Raiders of the Lost Ark*, and other classics.

• The Backstage Studio Tour takes you

behind the scenes at a movie studio. In the studio back lot, you see mock city streets, a make-believe earthquake, and more.

• At SuperStar Television, visitors act roles in famous TV shows. Then, through a little TV magic, they see themselves in the actual shows!

• At The Magic of Disney Animation, you can watch Disney artists at work on animated films. You learn just how these films are made.

There's much more to see and do, too. It all adds up to an exciting look at the magical world of movies and television.

The magic of special effects will put these girls in a movie. On film, they'll seem to fly through the air on the back of a giant bee.

PENCIL PALS

Do you ever have days when everything seems to go wrong? Well, just make friends with a pencil pal. Your pal will let everyone know if you're having a good day or a bad one!

To make your pal, you will need a pencil, a piece of long-haired fake fur, a pom-pom, ribbon, some wiggle eyes, and glue. (The fake fur and other materials can be bought at many craft and fabric stores.) Glue the fake fur around the top of the pencil. Then glue on the eyes and the pom-pom nose. Finally, tie on the ribbon and make a bow.

When you're happy, smooth the "hair" so that your pal looks content. But when you're upset, whirl the pencil between the palms of your hands. You pal's "hair" will go flying in all directions—reflecting your frazzled mood. Your pal may even cheer you up by getting you to smile!

A Meal Fit for a Cat

In a warehouse across the street from the Fat Cat Food Factory, Amelia Mouse stared at her empty cupboards. She had no food, but she couldn't let her children go hungry.

Amelia marched to the front door and looked out. There it was—a mousetrap with a fat piece of cheese. Fat Cat was there, too, waiting to pounce. But she had to get food!

She gave each of her children a hug. "If anything happens to me," she said, "call the Rescue Rangers. Understand?"

The children nodded. Then Amelia hurried out the door. She didn't get far.

Snap! The mousetrap closed on Amelia's tail.

"How nice," said Fat Cat, licking his lips. He dragged Amelia off to his office.

While his back was turned, the children sneaked out and ran for help.

Soon, at Rescue Rangers Headquarters, Chip heard squeaking at the door. When he opened it, he found the four young mice.

"Calm down!" said Chip. "One of you tell me what's going on!"

Dale joined Chip, and they listened while the oldest mouse explained.

"Fat Cat took over the warehouse where we live, so it's not safe anymore. But Mama went out anyway, and now Fat Cat's got her!" A tear slid down the young mouse's cheek.

"Don't worry," Chip said. "We'll save her!"

Chip pulled Dale inside. When they came out again, they looked like mice.

They left the children with Gadget, picked up Monterey Jack, and raced to the warehouse and crept inside.

"There's Fat Cat!" shouted Dale.

Chip put his hand over Dale's mouth. "Quiet!" he hissed.

Fat Cat was sitting at his dinner table. His

helpers were taking away the dirty dishes.

"I think I'll have Chocolate Mouse for dessert," said Fat Cat, laughing.

Monterey gulped. As he looked around for Amelia, he noticed some big containers against the wall marked "milk chocolate."

"We'd better find Amelia before she's dipped, mates!" said Monterey.

They stayed in the shadows and soon spotted Amelia in the corner, still pinned in the trap.

"All right, men," said Chip. "I'll get Fat Cat's attention while you free Amelia."

Chip scurried across the floor, just like a mouse, squeaking loudly.

"What was that?" asked Fat Cat.

Meanwhile, Dale and Monterey rushed to the trap, lifted the clamp, and freed Amelia.

"Thank goodness!" said Amelia.

"Okay," said Dale. "Let's get out of here!"

Amelia reached the door safely, but Monterey was standing frozen in place. He smelled something.

"Cheese!" cried
Monterey.

"Uh-oh," said
Chip, underneath
the table.

Fat Cat
turned and
saw Monterey Jack.

"You!" he growled. "The rest of those
Rescue Rangers must be here somewhere.
Get 'em, boys!"

Dale shook Monterey. "Snap out of it!" he
said.

Dale and Monterey took off. Chip ran out
from under the table to join them, and the
three headed for the street.

"Don't let them get away!" yelled Fat Cat.

Fat Cat and his helpers gave chase. Chip and Monterey made it to the door, but Fat Cat's paw slammed down on Dale's tail.

"Going somewhere?" asked Fat Cat.

"Oh, no!" said Chip.

When Amelia arrived alone at Rescue Ranger Headquarters, Gadget knew something was wrong. Telling Amelia to stay there with her children, Gadget grabbed her harpoon gun and some darts, snapped on her tool belt, and sped to the factory. She found Chip and Monterey outside.

"What happened?" asked Gadget. After Monterey had explained the situation, the three put their heads together

and came up with
a plan.

Gadget gave
Monterey the
harpoon gun, then
slipped inside.
Hiding behind a
stack of boxes, she
took out an old postage stamp. She rolled it
into a funnel shape and held it to her mouth
like a bullhorn.

"Hey, Big Boy," said Gadget, purring in
Fat Cat's direction. "Over here!"

While Fat Cat was distracted by the voice,
Chip and Monterey crept across the floor.

One of Fat Cat's helpers was holding Dale

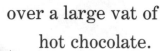

over a large vat of
hot chocolate.

Dale covered
his eyes,
afraid to
look down.
Monterey
aimed the harpoon
gun at the helper.
The dart hit his arm.

"Ow!" cried the helper, loosening his hold
on Dale. Dale felt himself slipping and
screamed.

Just then, Gadget left her hiding place and
headed straight for
the vat. Just as
she'd hoped, Fat
Cat took off after
her.

Monterey shot
a second dart. It
hit the helper's
hand, and he dropped
Dale just as Fat

Cat crashed into the vat, knocking it over.
Dale landed on Fat Cat's back and slid down
to the floor.

Chip and Monterey fought off Fat Cat and

his gang while Gadget ran to the door and
meowed at the top of her lungs.

Dale started the Rangermobile. "Come on!"
he called to Gadget. "What's taking so long?"

As Chip and Monterey used their last dart,
they all heard the one sweet sound they had

been waiting for—dogs barking.

"Quick!" called Dale. "Let's get out of here!"

Chip and Monterey raced outside, and all four took off in the Rangermobile just as a pack of dogs raced into the factory. As the Rescue Rangers rode away, they could hear Fat Cat and his gang screeching and scrambling to get away from the dogs.

When they got back to Ranger Head-quarters, Chip told Amelia, "You shouldn't

have any more problems with Fat Cat."

"I don't think he'll go back to *that* warehouse again," added Dale.

Amelia and the children thanked the Rangers and said good-bye.

That night, Chip made a pot of hot chocolate. "Want some?" he asked Dale.

"No, thanks!" said Dale, shaking his head. "If I *never* get near chocolate again, it'll be too soon!"

BODY TRICKS

Do you want to amaze your friends? Then play a few body tricks on them. All you need is a little knowledge about how the human body works. Then you can make your friends believe you are performing magic!

FLOATING ARMS

You can trick a friend and make him believe that his arms are floating up into the air at your command.

Ask your friend to stand in a doorway and push the backs of his hands against the door frame. Tell him to press as hard as he can while you count to 25. Then ask him to step quickly out of the doorway. As your friend moves forward, say: "Oh arms, I command you to rise." Your friend's arms will slowly float up in the air!

Why does this happen? Your friend's brain has been sending messages to his arms, telling them to press against the door frame. When he steps out of the doorway, his arms are still receiving these messages. And with nothing to press against, his arms rise.

SUPER FINGERS

Show a friend that your "super" fingers are stronger than her clenched fists. Ask her to press her fists together, one on top of the other. With your index fingers, quickly push her fists sideways, in opposite directions. Your friend isn't ready for force from the sides—she's pressing her fists up and down.

STICKY FINGERS

You can "glue" a friend's fingers together with magic! Ask him to form a steeple with his index fingers, pressing the knuckles of his other fingers together. Tell him to separate the index fingers (this will be easy). Have him do the same with his middle fingers. Finally, have him form a steeple with his ring fingers, and cast your spell. He won't be able to separate *these* fingers—the muscles in the ring fingers are too weak.

MAGIC WEIGHT

One minute, two friends can lift you. The next, it's impossible! First, put your hands on your shoulders, with your elbows pointing down. Ask two friends to stand on each side of you, and lift you by your elbows. This is easy. But now point your elbows straight in front of you and tell them to try again. Your friends won't be able to lift you by the elbows —no matter how hard they try.

This ocean animal is called a chambered nautilus. It builds a spiral shell, adding new "rooms" as it grows larger.

Twists of Nature

The spiral twists around and around, getting wider with each turn. This curving, swirling shape is one of the most beautiful forms in nature. And the spiral is one of the most common forms in nature, too. You can see spirals in plants and animals of all kinds.

Spirals can be seen in tiny one-celled animals. You can find them at the beach—in seashells. Spiral patterns can be found in larger animals, too. And in the plant world, spirals are everywhere. The leaves of many plants and the petals of many flowers are set in spiral patterns.

Scientists aren't sure why spirals are so common in nature. But spirals seem to be all around us. The next time you take a walk, look around. How many spirals can you find?

The spiral horns of a Dall sheep are powerful weapons. They also form a protective helmet.

Above: Dew outlines the true form of a spider's web—a dainty spiral spread in the branches of a tree. Below: The tendrils of a pumpkin vine uncurl in graceful spiral forms.

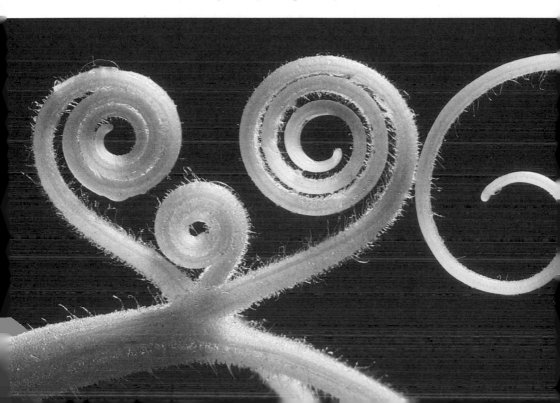

The Temple of Gloom

Mowgli was playing in a tall tree when he saw something white in the distance. It was the top of a very old stone tower.

"Let's go explore it," he called to his friends, Bagheera the panther and Baloo the bear.

"Oh, no, Mowgli." Bagheera shook his head. "Jungle folk never go near that tower. It is near the lost Temple of Gloom, where the terrible SadStone is hidden."

"SadStone?" laughed Mowgli. "So what?"

"It makes everyone who looks at it cry."

"Aw Baggie," said Baloo. "I don't believe all that old beeswax. And to prove it, I'll go there. So will Mowgli. We're not afraid."

So Mowgli and Baloo started for the tower, singing and laughing as they went.

They didn't know that Kaa, the python, was following them.

"Here'sss my chance to get my coils around Mowgli," Kaa said to himself.

"Baloo, it sounds like someone is following us," said Mowgli.

Kaa tried to look like a stick.

Baloo laughed. "It's probably Bagheera, trying to scare us," he said. "Don't pay any attention to him."

"Thisss is going to be easier than I thought," Kaa smiled slyly.

After a long walk, they found the tower. "This place gives me a funny feeling," Baloo said nervously. "And I don't mean a ha-ha funny feeling, either."

Mowgli laughed. "You're starting to sound just like Bagheera," he teased. "Come on, Baloo, where's your sense of humor?" He jumped on Baloo and started to tickle him.

Baloo laughed and wrestled Mowgli to the ground. They rolled in the leaves, mashing the end of Kaa's tail.

"That does it!" hissed Kaa. "I'm getting that Man-cub if it'sss the last thing I do!"

Baloo stood up. "I still don't like it here," he said. "Let's go." But Mowgli wanted to keep playing. He threw himself on Baloo again.

"Oof!" Baloo sat down hard. Suddenly a loud groaning sound filled the air. The ground shook, and a huge hole opened under Baloo.

"Help!" Baloo yelled as he toppled in.

Mowgli leaned over the edge of the hole. "Baloo! Are you all right?" he called.

"It's dark down here," called Baloo. "I can feel the walls, but I can't see anything."

Baloo touched something covered with mud. When he scraped some of the mud off, a bluish-white light began to glow.

Mowgli looked down. As he watched, he heard a funny sound. Baloo was sitting on the floor of the pit, holding an enormous blue jewel. And he was crying!

"Baloo! This must be the Temple of Gloom," Mowgli yelled. "And that's the SadStone!"

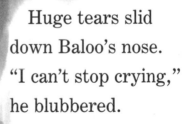

Huge tears slid down Baloo's nose. "I can't stop crying," he blubbered.

"Don't cry, Baloo! I'll get you out of there." Mowgli looked around for something to help Baloo climb out of the pit.

When Kaa saw that Mowgli was alone, he came out of hiding.

"What'sss the trouble," Kaa said as he approached Mowgli. He tried to make Mowgli look him in the eyes. "Can I help?"

Mowgli knew that if he looked Kaa in the eyes, Kaa would hypnotize him. Instead he looked at Kaa's long, long tail. And it gave him an idea.

"Oh, Kaa! I'm so glad to see you!" he said, still staring at Kaa's tail. As he talked, he slowly walked backward.

Kaa was pleased. No one was ever glad to see him. He slithered toward Mowgli. Mowgli backed up more. He began to walk around a tree trunk. Kaa followed every step.

"I'll bet there's no one in the jungle longer than you, Kaa," Mowgli said. He kept moving until Kaa's tail was wrapped around the tree.

"That'sss true," Kaa smiled.

Mowgli bent down and tied a huge knot in Kaa's tail. Kaa was fastened to the tree!

"Why, you little shrimp!" Kaa hissed. "I'll get you for that!"

Mowgli grabbed a vine and swung out over the deep pit where Baloo sat crying.

Kaa lunged, straight out over the pit.

"Aaahhhh!" Kaa screeched as he crashed into the pit. There he hung, upside down, with his tail tied firmly to the tree.

"Quick, Baloo!" Mowgli called. "Throw me the SadStone. Then climb up Kaa like a rope."

Still sniffling, Baloo threw the SadStone out of the pit. Then he began to climb up Kaa. Baloo's big furry paws tickled Kaa's back. Soon the python was giggling helplessly.

"Oooh, hee-hee-hee! That tickles! Get off, you big bag of fuzz!" Kaa sounded so funny Baloo started to laugh. When he reached the top of the pit, his tears were gone.

"Now what will we do with Kaa?" said Baloo. "We can't just leave him hanging."

"Kaa won't bother us for a while," Mowgli smiled. "Help me pull him up."

Together Baloo and Mowgli pulled Kaa up.
Then, being careful not to look at the
SadStone himself, Mowgli held it in front of
Kaa's eyes while Baloo untied Kaa's tail.

"You're free now, Kaa," Mowgli said. But
Kaa didn't care. He was staring at the Sad-
Stone. First he sighed, then he sniffled. Then
he burst into huge, scaly tears. And then Kaa
slithered away into the jungle, wailing loudly.

Mowgli tossed the SadStone back into the
pit. "Let's leave it there, where it can't make
anyone else cry," he said. Then he and Baloo
started home.

Bagheera met them on their way. "Well?"
he asked. "What happened?"

"Nothing," Mowgli answered. He winked
at Baloo. "Nothing worth crying about."

THE FUN OF
FADS

"Smile" faces, like the blushing grin on the button at left, and Hula-Hoops, below, are old fads that were popular again in 1989.

*Skateboarding began as a fad in the 1960's.
Now millions of people are doing it!*

Every year seems to have its fads—toys
and activities that suddenly are all the rage
and just as quickly go out again.

There were plenty of fads in the 1980's.
Children collected stickers. They also
collected Cabbage Patch Kids, which were so
popular that their manufacturer couldn't

For a while, Cabbage Patch Kids were so popular that kids waited months to get one.

make enough of the dolls. And some fads of the past returned. The "smile" face was a fad of the 1970's. In 1989, it was back—on everything from buttons to clothes. The Hula-Hoop, a toy that was a fad in the 1950's, was also popular again.

How do fads get started? Some are dreamed up by toy makers. The Hula-Hoop was developed by a toy company that heard of children using bamboo hoops in exercise classes. The company started making hoops in bright plastic. And by the late 1950's, they were everywhere.

Some fads have staying power. Skateboarding began as a fad in the 1960's. Now millions of people are doing it. But some fads are just silly. One of the biggest fads of the 1970's was the Pet Rock. It was nothing more than a rock in a box!

Why do such silly fads take hold? The most likely reason is a simple one: Fads are fun!

The Pet Rock was just a rock in a box. Would you have guessed that it would be one of the biggest fads of the 1970's?

Pop Goes the Page

Open one of these books, and—surprise! The pictures slide, jiggle, turn, and jump right off the page.

Today's pop-up books include Hot Pursuit *(above) and* Lavinia's Cottage *(below). The* Human Body *(right) shows how the body works.*

These are pop-up and movable books. And they have been made for hundreds of years. Some of the earliest ones were made in the 1500's. They were used to teach adults about the night sky. They had revolving disks and pointers to show the positions of the stars.

In the 1800's, many pop-up books were made for children. Fairy tales were a favorite subject. Today pop-up books of all kinds are popular once again. And as always, they are full of surprises!

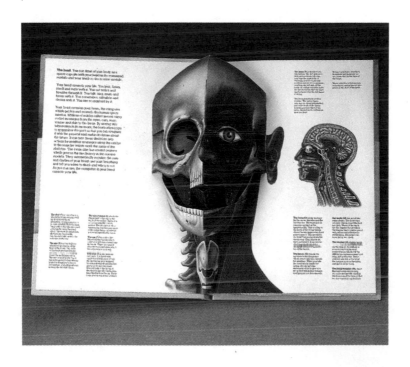

A group of meerkats enjoys a sunbath. These clever little animals can stand up for hours.

United They Stand

The meerkat is a little African animal with an unusual ability: It can stand upright on its hind legs. In fact, meerkats can stand upright for hours. The pose looks comical—but it's one of the tricks that these clever animals use to survive.

Meerkats are relatives of the mongoose. They are about the size of squirrels, and they live in the hot, dry plains of southern Africa. Life there is hard. But meerkats manage— through teamwork. These animals live together in underground burrows. And they work together in every part of life, from finding food to raising their young.

A band of meerkats spends most of the day searching for insects, eggs, plant bulbs, and

A meerkat acts as a guard for the rest of the colony. It stands on its hind legs, using its tail as a brace. It is always aware of danger. Sometimes an alert meerkat can't even finish its dinner!

other food. Most of the meerkats scurry around on all fours, sniffing and scratching the dry ground. But one meerkat always acts as a guard. That's where the upright stance comes in handy. The guard meerkat stands up and scans the area for jackals, eagles, and other enemies. If the guard senses danger, it warns the others with a peep or a bark.

Meerkats even work together in raising their young. When a mother meerkat goes out to hunt for food; one of the other adults stays behind. This meerkat acts as a babysitter for the youngsters until the mother returns.

"Say a few words for your fans," a scientist seems to ask a meerkat. Scientists are studying these animals to learn more about them.

The meerkats take turns on guard duty. That way, all have a chance to eat. Adult meerkats also take turns cuddling and grooming baby meerkats. They may even act as babysitters, so that a mother meerkat can go hunting for food! These clever and comical animals have found that teamwork is the secret to survival in their harsh world.

The Loch Mess Monster

Scrooge McDuck checked his scuba gear.
He was getting ready to go after the Loch
Mess Monster as his nephews were rowing
the boat to the middle of Loch Mess.

"All ready, boys!" said Scrooge. "Now all
we have to do is wait for Messy to show her
pretty face."

"How do you know she will, Uncle
Scrooge?" asked Webby.

"She has been seen every sundown at this
time for a week," replied Scrooge. "And then
a sheep disappears. She'll be here tonight."

Scrooge smiled as he thought of the money he would make once he had captured Messy. Some museum would pay a fortune for a living dinosaur. The villagers would reward him, too, for getting rid of the sheep-stealing monster for them.

"Do you remember the plan, boys?" asked Scrooge.

Huey, Dewey, and Louie repeated the steps. "First Uncle Scrooge dives in and ties this rope to her tail," said Louie, holding up a piece of strong rope that was attached to the boat.

"Then Messy will tow us to her hideout while Uncle Scrooge follows," Dewey added.

"And when we know where she hides, we can come back and capture her," said Huey.

Suddenly the boat began to rock back and forth. In the fading light, Louie saw a dark shape coming straight for them.

"Get ready, Uncle Scrooge!" Webby called. "Something's coming." Scrooge took the rope and jumped over the side of the boat.

As the dark shape got closer, the boat began to rock.

"It's coming right for us!" yelled Louie.
"Everyone hold on tight!"

The dinosaur swept past them. The rope
began to uncoil. The little boat jumped
forward and began to bump across the lake.

"Uncle Scrooge must have roped her!"
yelled Louie. Suddenly the boat crashed to a
halt. All four ducks piled up in the bow of the
boat.

"What a ride!" gasped Huey, sitting up.
"Where are we?" They peered carefully over
the side of the boat, only to find they were on
the shore.

"Where's Messy?" asked Louie.

"Where's Uncle Scrooge?" asked Webby.

"Oh, he'll be all right," said Dewey, "but I'm worried about us. It's dark, and we don't know where we are."

They decided to make camp. Then Louie went to look for firewood.

"Hey! Come here!" shouted Louie. The others followed his voice and found him near the mouth of a cave.

After a quick search, they found a lantern and some matches. In minutes, the lantern was shining brightly.

"Wow!" said Huey. "Look at all this stuff."

There were bicycle pumps, cans of spray paint, and big car inner tubes lying around the floor of the cave.

But Webby found the biggest surprise—seven big, beautiful sheep, all tied together. "These must be the missing sheep," she said.

"Something fishy is going on here," said Dewey.

"Yeah," said Louie. "And I don't think it has anything at all to do with a sheep-stealing sea monster."

"You got that right," said a familiar voice. They turned and saw four figures standing at the cave entrance, holding a string of inner tubes painted to look like a monster and leading a frightened sheep.

"The Beagle Boys!" gasped Huey. "You're the ones who have been stealing the sheep. You use a fake monster to make the villagers think it was Messy."

"Grab them," Big Time ordered. The other three Beagles caught the boys, but Webby got away. In seconds, she had disappeared down a dark tunnel.

"Let her go," said Bouncer. "She'll be back. There's no other way out of the cave."

"You'll never get away with this!" yelled Louie, as Big Time tied them up.

"Who's going to stop us?" Big Time grinned. "While the villagers are looking for a sea monster, we'll be driving their prize sheep to the auction. We'll make a bundle!"

After the boys were tied up, the Beagles began to load the sheep into a truck. Suddenly an eerie sound stopped them.

"What was that?" Baggy whispered, looking toward the tunnel where Webby had disappeared. A second noise sent the Beagles out of the cave on the run. All except Big Time. He reached behind a bale of hay and pulled out a small, wet figure.

"Scrooge McDuck!" he barked. "What're you doin' here, makin' monster noises?"

Seeing it was only Scrooge, the other Beagles went back to work. Big Time tied Scrooge up and left him with his nephews.

As the last sheep went into the truck, they heard a roar from the mouth of the tunnel. Then a giant shadow fell across the truck. "What's that?" asked Baggy.

There was another roar, and a real, live sea
monster stepped from the tunnel, with
Webby on her back.

"Get 'em, Messy!" she ordered.

"Run!" Big Time yelled. But they were no
match for Messy. One flick of her gigantic tail
knocked them off their feet.
Webby slid off Messy's back and
freed the boys and Scrooge.
Together they tied up
the Beagle Boys and
loaded them into the
truck.

"Oh, Uncle Scrooge," said Webby. "I was so worried about you! What happened after you jumped into the water?"

"I grabbed the rope and Messy pulled me right into an underwater entrance to this cave," he explained. "Then I lost her. I wandered around until I found the boys here and tried to scare the Beagles away."

"But it was Messy who really did the scaring," said Webby, patting the dinosaur. "Now that she's rescued us, you won't really sell her to a museum, will you, Uncle Scrooge?"

"No! I couldn't do that. Messy's secret will be safe with me." Messy leaned over and gave Scrooge a big kiss.

"Phew!" said Scrooge. "She smells like fish."

"Well, what did you expect from a real, live Plesiosaur?" giggled Webby. "They don't really eat sheep, you know."

ZAP!

Lightning can travel from one cloud to another—or from a cloud to the ground.

ZAP! A flash of lightning zigzags across the sky. A second later, the boom and rumble of thunder reaches your ears.

Lightning strikes millions of times each day, all around the world. A lightning flash is really a huge spark of electricity. The spark creates a shock wave in the air. And you hear the shock wave as thunder.

Lightning is exciting—but dangerous. When you see thunder clouds, stay indoors!

Ben Franklin flew a kite in a thunderstorm. He felt electricity travel down the string to a metal key that was attached to it. He proved that lightning is electricity. But he was lucky—he could have been killed!

A Connecticut team scored the first U.S. win in the Little League World Series since 1983.

PLAY BALL!

"Play ball!" Every spring, millions of kids grab bats, mitts, and balls and run out to the nearest baseball diamond to answer that call. So do millions of adults. In fact, baseball has been called "America's national pastime." And 1989 was an important year for the game.

First, baseball celebrated its 150th

birthday in 1989. Legend has it that the game was invented in 1839 by a man named Abner Doubleday, in Cooperstown, New York. Many historians don't think the story is true. But baseball fans celebrated the date all the same.

It was also the 50th birthday of Little League Baseball, the organized league for

In 1989, Victoria Brucker became the first U.S. girl to play in a Little League World Series. The 12-year-old player from San Pedro, California, scored several runs for her team.

players 6 to 18 years old. Little League began in 1939 in Williamsport, Pennsylvania. Back then, there were just three local teams. Today there are thousands of Little League teams in 34 countries.

U.S. Little Leaguers had an especially exciting year. Since 1983, teams from other countries have won the Little League World Series, held in Williamsport each year. But in 1989 a team from Trumbull, Connecticut, beat a team from Taiwan to win the Series.

The 1989 Little League World Series also saw an important first. Victoria Brucker, a 12-year-old player on a team from San Pedro, California, became the first U.S. girl to play in the championship. (Girls have played on Little League teams since 1974, but none had reached the Series.) During the year Little League also started a new division for handicapped players.

Many major league baseball players got their start in Little League. Will today's Little League players be the baseball stars of tomorrow?

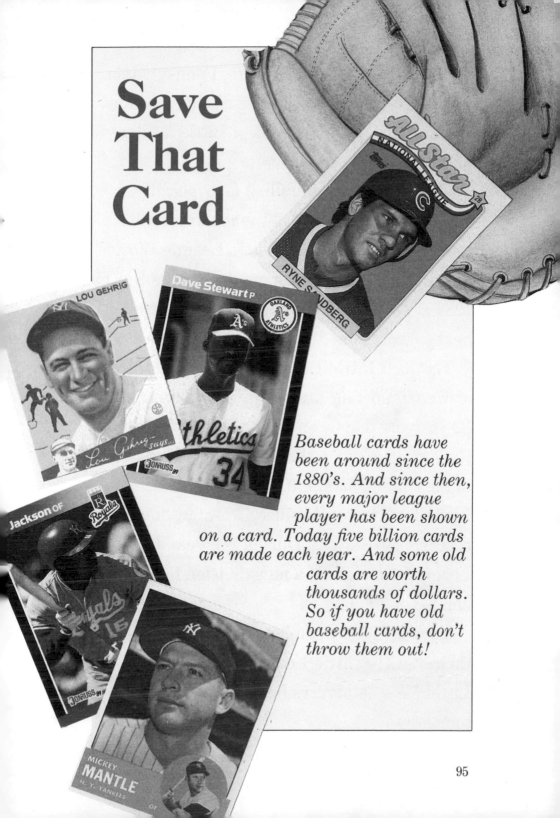

Save That Card

Baseball cards have been around since the 1880's. And since then, every major league player has been shown on a card. Today five billion cards are made each year. And some old cards are worth thousands of dollars. So if you have old baseball cards, don't throw them out!